Self Confidence Secrets

How To Be
Outgoing
and
Overcome
Shyness

Lucas McCain

Laurenzana Press

Published by:
Laurenzana Press
PO Box 1220
Melrose, FL 32666 USA

www.LaurenzanaPress.com

ISBN-13 : 978-1-937918-54-5

Table of Contents

How Confident Are You?

How confident would you say you are? Are you shy or easily intimidated? Are you a wallflower who feels socially awkward?

If you struggle with self-confidence, you may tell yourself that it doesn't matter. The truth is, although the world can be tough on people who lack confidence, improving your self-image and eliminating negative self-talk can improve your life in a variety of ways.

Self-Confidence Makes People Happier

You might assume that confident people are generally happier than those who lack self-esteem. But did you know that confident people actually believe they deserve happiness? And as a result they are more likely to make efforts to improve bad moods or situations than their less confident counterparts.

Not convinced? The Social Science and Humanities Research Council of Canada funded a study on the link between self-confidence, happiness, and mood management. Conducted by Professor Joanne Wood, and graduate students Sara Heimpel and Margaret Marshall, the study examined the confidence level of 900, and how likely they were to try to improve their moods or situations when confronted with sad news.

The researchers concluded that approximately 77% of the people with high self-esteem took initiatives to improve their moods; whereas only 55% of the people with low self-esteem tried to improve their behavior. The general consensus of the people with low self-esteem was that they deserved to feel bad. Whereas the individuals with high self-esteem had no doubt that things were likely to get better.

Self-confidence Improves Chances for Success

Did you know that confident people have more success at getting and keeping jobs? That may sound intuitive, but it's also scientifically proven to be true.

Jeylan Mortimer of the University of Minnesota, Mike Vuolo of Purdue University, and Jeremy Staff of Pennsylvania State University analyzed data dating back to 1988 from over 1,000 adolescents who answered questions about confidence and career aspirations when they were in high school.

The subjects were followed as they aged, and the research determined that the students who had reported high levels of confidence and career aspirations in their adolescence were more likely to be employed before, during and after their more adult years.

The Secret of Self-Confidence

What makes people confident? Is it being the prettiest woman or the richest man? It turns out that self-confidence is linked to specific factors, many of which are beyond people's control.

This guide will talk about self-compassion (being kind to yourself), self-talk (what stories you tell yourself), and social comparison (why comparing yourself to others can hurt or help your self-esteem).

You'll also learn how to achieve the level of confidence you desire, using only the factors under your control with no gimmicks, scientifically-backed psychology, and basic tools everyone has at their disposal.

To truly live a happier, more fulfilling life, you need to learn the confidence practices described within. This program is designed such that you can read through the guide once, then re-read to put each principle into practice.

You are encouraged to start a confidence journal and tackle one practice each week, cycling through the 21 principles over the upcoming year. Once you've mastered these exercises, you'll experience significant boosts in your confidence level regardless of your circumstances.

Make note of which exercises work the best for you, and look for ways to continue them for the rest of your life. Feel free to explore variations of the recommended practices as you may find your own versions work best for you, and you can custom design your own program with the tools that resonate with your personality and needs.

In any case, it is hoped that you come away from this effort feeling empowered and confident!

Attention All Eagle Eyes: We've had a number of people proof this book before we released it to you, but there is a chance you might spot something that was missed. If you find a typo or other obvious error, please send it to us. If you're the first one to report it, we'll send you a free gift! Please send to: corrections@laurenzanapress.com

---

Admire, Adore, and Affirm Yourself Every Day

Does this title seem extravagant or narcissistic? You'd better get used to it, because this is the affirmation exercises you'll be practicing every day for the duration of the program as it's the most effective tool of all.

Much of your self-confidence relies on self-perception. If you perceive yourself as incompetent, inadequate or inferior in some way, your confidence will plummet. However, if you can change your perspective so that you perceive yourself as competent, adequate, and superior, your self-confidence will soar.

What is "self-perception"? Many people think they have to be competent and/or superior to have a good self-image. But studies have shown that the only thing that really matters is what people believe to be true about themselves. A beautiful woman can perceive herself as ugly and inadequate. An idiotic man can perceive himself as brilliant, and feel superior to the rest of the world. Therefore, what people believe to be their reality (self-perception) is what really matters.

Several studies have supported the theory that what people believe to be true about themselves is fundamental to their level of self-confidence. One such study published in the January 2009 *Journal of Psychology of Sport and Exercise* evaluated tennis players who were taught to deliberately change their self-talk. The players, regardless of ability, experienced an increase in self-confidence, and a decrease in performance anxiety over the course of five sessions.

Does that mean you should trick your mind into believing you are a better, more competent person than you really are? Not at all. Nevertheless, people take cues from a variety of sources when trying to determine how they should feel what they project to the world. Much as people try to resist outside influences, some or all of the following can sway one's self-perception:

- What other people say directly and indirectly.
- How they react in a close-knit environment (nonverbal communication).
- How strong and infallible their relationships are (people who are trusted the most are often the most influential on behavior).
- How they are scored and judged on their skills and intelligence.
- How they perceive people depicted in the media.

Unwittingly, social cues often dictate who a person chooses to be and what they feel their self-worth is. Social influences feed a person's self-perception, thereby making it difficult for them to feel good about themselves if those cues are sending negative messages.

Some people are better at ignoring these prompts than others. This guide will focus on adjusting your self-perception since it affects something equally as important to your overall well-being: Self-Talk.

Why Does Self-Talk Matter?

Much of how people feel about themselves is directly affected by the positive or negative words they use. For example, imagine you're having your neighbors over for dinner for the first time and you burned the rice. How you feel about yourself in that moment can be affected by a significant choice you make:

- **Self-deprecation:** I am so stupid! I always try to take shortcuts, which is why I constantly screw things up. My house smells like burned rice, they're going to hate dinner because I have nothing to serve with the vegetables, and they're going to dislike me because I'm a bad hostess and a rotten cook.

- **Positive affirmation:** I should have been more careful, but if I put this pot of rice outside it'll smell okay inside. I'm going tell them the story, they'll think it's funny, and will be fine with my suggestion to order pizza or go out for dinner. Maybe they prefer eating low-carb and would want just the vegetables without the rice. I might be serving something they'd actually want to eat.

As you can guess, the second response is much better for your self-esteem than the first.

Self-Talk That Works

Your self-esteem won't change if you tell yourself lies. Telling yourself "I'm the most handsome man [or most beautiful woman] in the world" when you know it isn't the truth won't help you feel better about yourself at all. Hearing "I'm a beautiful human being with a gift for passion, compassion, and humanity" will speak to the truth of your spirit.

Unfortunately, people are more prone to believing negative things about themselves. They can say "I'm so stupid" or "I'm so clumsy," and will accept such exaggerations to be true because it's easier to believe negative suggestions than positive ones.

You may have had a painfully humbling, and embarrassing experience that has kept you immobilized and not wanting to re-experience those negative emotions. For example, you thought you were going to win that spelling bee back in third grade. But you were eliminated in the second round, and you're afraid to think of yourself as smarter than what your subconscious tells you.

However, you can overcome these tendencies to put yourself down if you focus on genuine, positive attributes you know to be true. Believable, truthful affirmations are critical, because they are the foundation upon which you build your confidence. Once a strong foundation of self-confidence is established, you can avoid thinking negative thoughts that can sabotage your self-esteem.

Daily Challenge for Week One:
Things You Like About Yourself

First, you need to write down certain qualities you love about yourself. Start with the big attributes and work your way down to less significant things (write down things you know in your soul to be true). Your list might look like:

- I am kind and humanitarian, especially to those in need or who are weak
- I am hard-working
- I am truth worthy
- I am responsible, and people can count on me
- I am polite
- I am attractive
- I am funny
- I am usually on time
- I am a good pet owner
- I have a tidy home

Once you've made this list, spend time re-reading it and enjoying the truths you've listed.

Going forward you have a challenge to daily add three things you genuinely like about yourself (they can be important or small). What matters is that you believe them to be true, and that you feel good about yourself as you write them down. Your daily list can be the same or different each day – it doesn't matter. Just be sure it reflects the truth about you on that particular day.

Your daily list of three truths may look like this:

- I did the dishes before I left for work. This makes me feel good about being a responsible, conscientious partner and homeowner.

- I walked the dog for 30 minutes. This makes me feel good about being a kind pet owner and a person who exercises to be healthy.

- I held my tongue when my boss was being rude. This makes me feel good about being someone who has the self-control not to snipe when other people are inconsiderate. It also means I am professional and wise about when to fight and when to turn the other cheek.

You'll do this exercise every day for the duration of the program (and hopefully for the rest of your life) along with your list of other tasks.

Focusing on things you like about yourself and writing them down will help build a solid foundation of good self-esteem.

Baby Yourself

Week one was about building a solid foundation based on things you truly like about yourself. This week's focus is self-talk – the most powerful component of building confidence – and how to defend yourself against negative, internal dialogue.

Of course it would be nice if you could brush away negative thoughts like a piece of lint on a sweater, but the psyche of human beings isn't constructed that way. Psychologists speculate that people learn to focus on the negative in order to avoid anything that might hurt them, and thus the need for survival. Unfortunately, that means fears and negative feelings can be exaggerated and become obsessive, which leads to spiraling downward into an emotional pit of despair.

However, people who are compassionate about themselves – babying if you will – tend to rebound from disappointment and discouragement sooner than those who chastise themselves for failure.

A study conducted by researchers at Duke and Wake Forest Universities (May 2007 issue of the *Journal of*

Personality and Social Psychology) concludes that this is a helpful strategy for people with low self-esteem.

How to Defend Yourself Against Negative Self-Talk

It may help to think about your ego as a small, vulnerable child who can easily be fooled. If you have the opportunity to be around children, watch how easily they can be manipulated. If you tell them an ice cream cone is called a lollipop, they'll call it a lollipop. If you tell a child they are stupid, chances are they will believe they are stupid.

A child can be psychologically damaged the longer they believe negative talk given to them by someone they trust such as a parent, teacher or a peer at school. Their vulnerability sets the stage for mental abuse and implants they will carry with them their entire life.

Your ego is much like a naïve child, so you need to learn how to protect it just like you'd protect a little one. Many people who have low self-esteem have not learned how to defend themselves against negative self-talk. So this week we're going to teach you this invaluable skill.

The Power of Self-Talk

Whenever you think negatively about yourself, you'll need to have the tools to switch your mindset to positive self-talk (clinically referred to as "cognitive behavioral therapy") to protect your self-esteem.

Dr. David Burns, author of *Feeling Good*, uses self-talk and rationalization to help patients overcome negative feelings such a guilt and shame. He calls his special form of cognitive behavior therapy "avoiding cognitive distortions," and instructs his patients do something like: "Let's say you've been good about sticking to a diet to lose weight. You went to McDonald's one night, ate way too much at a party the next night, and now you're feeling guilty and are upset with yourself."

Dr. Burns would have you do a question and answer session with yourself such as:

Q: *What do I feel bad about?*

A: *I went off my diet. I ate junk food one night and too much at a party the next night.*

Q: *What negative self-talk am I telling myself?*

A: *I'm fat, undisciplined, and unlovable.*

The Truth Behind Your Negative Thoughts

You'll need to think rationally about each one of your negative thoughts and come to truth-based solutions. Again, you should think of your ego as a small child, and help it evaluate the negative thoughts, find solutions, and get back on track emotionally.

You need to have an objective, logical estimation of your situation, so ask yourself pertinent questions and answer them as honestly as possible to assess the reality of your thoughts and fears.

Negative Thought 1: I went off my diet

a. *Is it normal for dieters to fall off the wagon? Yes. Most dieters cannot stick to their regimen for very long.*

b. *Can I get back on my diet? Of course you can. It's completely normal to have setbacks several times while dieting.*

Negative Thought 2: I'm fat, undisciplined, and unloved

a. *I am overweight in comparison to whom? The whole world? My sister?*

b. *What is my ideal weight or my ideal BMI (body mass index)?*

c. *Am I really all that undisciplined? Have I always been undisciplined? In what areas I am disciplined?*

Look for areas where you've had self-control. Perhaps you're good at returning calls or emails, keeping up with the bills, or accomplishing tasks at work. Maybe you're a fabulous mother or grandmother, or a great coach. To get a proper perspective of yourself you need to tell your subconscious that if you are disciplined in a particular area, you can be disciplined with anything. It just takes time and training.

Negative Thought 3: I'm unlovable because I'm fat and undisciplined.

a. *Do I love anyone who is overweight?*

b.   Do I love anyone who is undisciplined?

c.   What does being overweight or undisciplined have to do with lovability?

d.   Do I know anyone who is overweight or undisciplined who is in a healthy relationship?

You need to understand that such factors don't apply just to you; but that they're normal struggles shared by many people who are loved, respected and much cherished.

Repeat your question and answer sessions until you can let go of the shame, self-deprecation or guilt, and plan a positive future outcome. If the situations trigger feelings of guilt or self-loathing, you might ask a trusted friend to help you approach them rationally (and please – be gentle with yourself!).

Daily Challenge for Week Two:

A Cognitive Behavior Therapy Chart

Prepare yourself ahead of time for bad days by having the following list at your beck and call:

- What I feel bad about
- Negative thoughts I'm having
- Rational questions to ask myself
- The truth about the situation and about me

Type or write them out long-hand, and leave room for the answers. Place copies into your journal or in a safe place for future use. If something bad happens this week, you can start using the chart. (This exercise will be continued every week for the duration of the course.)

By week two you will:

- Record three things you like about yourself every day.
- Have at your disposal a Cognitive Behavior Therapy Chart to track what occurs on bad days.

Cultivate Caring Connections

Self-confidence is rooted in the quality of people's relationships. According to a University of Michigan School of Nursing study, a sense of belonging and having close relationships makes a significant difference in mental and emotional health. This includes how confident, happy or depressed a person feels.

Relationships make people feel safe and worthy of attention, which strengthens them emotionally. If they have emotionally satisfying relationships, they are able to deflect feelings of inadequacy more easily than if their social connections are weak.

Find a Safe Relationship

The world can be brutal. Co-workers can be catty and competitive, neighbors can be judgmental, and relatives can be critical and alienating. Such critics make it necessary to find relationships or communities where it's safe to be genuinely emotionally connected.

Take some time now to write out a list of your social connections. After you've written down names of individuals and groups, answer the following questions:

- Can I be myself with this person or group?
- Can I be open about my struggles, fears, or weaknesses?
- Can I show up as I am without fearing judgment or criticism?
- Do I laugh easily with this person or group?
- When I am done spending time with this person or group, do I feel refreshed or drained?
- Do I want to be around them in the future?

Now identify which people or groups feel like your safest relationships.

Some people get hurt because they assume all relationships are safe and reveal too much about themselves. Because they have set themselves up to be vulnerable, when the relationship proves not to be safe they get hurt.

Some good candidates for safe relationships are:

- A sibling or friend who "gets" you
- A neighbor who makes you laugh
- A co-worker who always has your back no matter that happens
- A friend who is open about their problems and listens to yours

- An AA or NA group
- A church community
- A book club with members who share your world view

Transforming a Shallow Relationship Into a Safe Relationship

If you feel like you aren't connecting emotionally with people, you may want to start "dating" someone to see if they're a good candidate for a safe relationship. Take the following steps as you investigate the depth of a possible connection:

- Initiate time alone together.

- Share something personal and see how the person responds. Are they supportive or judgmental? How did you feel after sharing your information with them?

- Ask them about their life to see if they will share openly with you.

- Ask them if they would be willing to connect more often. Set a second time for another phone call, email, or time together, then see if they follow through or cancel.

- If they look like they will make you a priority, keep building the relationship. If it doesn't seem to be working, move on to another possibility.

Daily Challenge for Week Three:

Set aside time to commit to this important social support network. If you have close relationships, schedule appointments with one or more of your safe associates this week.

If you don't have safe friendships, make a list of possibilities of people or groups and begin the process to connect. If you think a community event would be ideal, visit a book club, AA group, NA group, church, or other close-knit setting.

If you're more comfortable writing or talking on the phone than meeting in person (at least at first), initiate a safe relationship with someone via these methods.

By week three you will:

- Record three things you like about yourself every day.
- Track what occurs on bad days in your Cognitive Behavior Therapy Chart.
- Begin establishing a social support network.

Dare to Be Different

"Decide if fitting in is more important than finding out what you're doing here."

Eve Ensler

Parents try to teach children to be proud of who they are, and that they shouldn't be afraid to be different. This theme is consistently found in books, movies, and songs. However, many adults still haven't figured out who they are and how to proudly live as a "different" individual. They compare themselves to the standards and expectations set forth by society (or engrained in them as children).

They try to be "normal" by living up to unreasonable standards that lead to emotional exhaustion and a sense they can never do enough, be enough, or perform well enough. Every time people compare themselves to others, they risk damaging their self-esteem and confidence.

The Psychology of Living Authentically

Living authentically refers to living your life in a way that pleases you, and is not restricted by the standards and expectations of others.

How to Live Your Life Authentically

"Tell me, what is it you plan to do
with your one wild and precious life?"

Mary Oliver

To determine how you are/are not living authentically, you need to evaluate several aspects of your life. Because the focus of this program is on increasing self-confidence, you'll want to focus not only on what makes you happiest, but what rings true with your authentic self.

Authentic Living Exercise

Answer the following questions, and look for areas that do not align with your authenticity. Flag answers that indicate you're trying to be someone other than your true self.

At Home

- Does your living space reflect who you are?
- Do you live in the type of home or apartment that reflects your values and personality?
- Do you consistently perform tasks (housecleaning, landscaping, yard work) that feel burdensome or you "have to do it to be respected"?
- What would your ideal home look and feel like?

At Work

- Does your job reflect your potential?

- Do you get to use your talents and strengths?
- Do you feel satisfied when you complete work tasks?
- Does your work environment nurture you?
- Would you be happier working at home, or in an office with fewer or more co-workers?

Personal Style

- Do you dress to match the latest styles or to suit your preferences?
- Do you feel your clothing and accessories reflect who you are?
- Is there someone you respect because they dress to reflect their personality more adequately than you do?
- How could you express yourself more accurately through your personal style?

Personal Beliefs

- Do you attend a club or church to please others?
- Are you genuinely benefitting from the groups to which you belong?
- Do you have to bite your tongue to avoid offending others?
- Do you surround yourself with people who view the world the same way you do?
- How could you meet more people who share your beliefs and views?

Schedule

- Do you honor your body's natural clock?

- Do you force yourself to live a schedule that doesn't work for you?

- Is your schedule too full or not full enough?

- Do you find yourself wasting hours watching television or surfing the Web?

- Do you always feel rushed, overtired, overworked?

- Is there any way you could alter your schedule to better suit your body's needs?

Lifestyle

- Do you make time for the activities that nurture your soul?

- Are you committed to activities you feel you have to do or should do?

- Are you living a traditional, conventional lifestyle when you feel you are better suited to an alternative lifestyle?

- What would your ideal lifestyle look like, and how could you transition to this new lifestyle?

Daily Challenge for Week Four:

Complete the Living Authentically Exercise and Begin Making Changes

To complete this exercise, you'll need to break it into specific journal entries to accomplish over the course of the week. As you answer the questions, try to think outside of the box. What changes will you/could you make to help yourself start living authentically? You might decide to make some big changes such as:

- Moving to a different city or country
- Selling your home
- Changing career paths
- Ending a relationship or starting a new relationship
- Quitting a church, community organization, or club
- Starting a new club

If you're uncomfortable working your way up to bigger changes, you might start with smaller changes such as:

- No longer wearing make-up
- Getting a new haircut
- Wearing glasses instead of contacts
- Giving away clothes that no longer suit you, and shopping for clothing that fit your personality

- Planting wildflowers instead of conventional landscaping
- Adopting a pet
- Asking your boss if you can work virtually from home instead of going into the office each day
- Or changing your work schedule so you go in at 10:00am and work until 6:30pm, instead of trying to work 8:30 to 5:00 each day

Whatever you do, this is the week to evaluate your life and decide what changes would make you feel happier. The goal here is to honor your authentic self, including your taste and preferences.

By week four you will:

- Record three things you like about yourself every day.
- Track what occurs on bad days in your Cognitive Behavior Therapy Chart.
- Begin establishing a social support network.
- Write out the answers to the questions in the exercise, and identify changes you'd like to make to honor your true self.

Express Yourself

When people suffer from low self-esteem, they often find it difficult to effectively defend or speak up for themselves.

Dr. Harriet Lerner, author of *The Dance of Anger*, *The Dance of Fear*, and *The Dance of Intimacy*, describes an all-too-common communication problem: When people are insecure or lack confidence, they find themselves submitting out of a desire to please others. They may say yes when they should say no, or acquiesce when they don't agree with something. Then when they can't take it anymore they explode, and act out negatively with anger or distress. This all-or-nothing style of communication is common for people who lack confidence.

If you find yourself falling into any of these communication traps, you probably feel like people don't respect you. When you submit, people can take advantage of you. And when you blow up or fall apart and cry, people won't take you seriously or temporarily placate you. You need to learn how to communicate calmly, clearly and confidently in order to have people respect your opinions.

Learning How to Express Yourself Confidently

Learning to speak confidently entails thinking confidently and practicing your lines before speaking. These two simple steps will help you make great strides as you begin to express yourself more often and with more authority.

Step One: Allow Yourself Time to Think

Instead of rushing to respond, ask for time. Don't say yes when asked to do something; respond instead with "I'll get back to you on that." If someone zings you with an insult or a jab, respond with silence or an excuse to get some time to think before responding.

When people lack confidences, they can't think clearly when presented with conflict or a decision. Their natural instinct is to acquiesce so they will be liked or appreciated. A typical fighting back instinct (if a person hasn't treated them well or they have given in too many times in the past) is to say something in anger.

You need time to think so you can break any negative patterns. It's a good idea to come up with a few standard responses to buy you time to think before responding. Some good examples are:

- I'm busy right now, but I'll get back to you on that.
- Give me a minute.
- Let me think it over.
- I'm not so sure about that, but I'll let you know.
- Let me check my schedule.

Step Two: Your Opinion is Valid

Now that you've got a minute to think before responding, check in with yourself to determine how you really feel. Affirm your right to express how you really feel and that you deserve to have your opinions heard and respected.

Now ask yourself questions about the actual incident:

- Is this a commitment you really want to make?
- How does the commitment make you feel?
- If you're responding to an insult or jab, did they really mean to insult you? Or were you taking the comment too seriously?
- What else could this person have meant by that statement?
- How did the insult or jab make you feel?
- What do you really want to communicate to this person? Is it worth the conflict?
- Do you have any other options?

Step Three: Practice Your Lines Before Speaking

Once you've determined your answer, practice your lines since you've been given more time. You can write them down or practice them in your head. Identify exactly what you want to communicate, and focus on the correct delivery of your words. You must practice saying the lines clearly and with confidence.

You'll be surprised at how effective direct communication can be, especially when it's delivered calmly and with authority. Use phrases like:

- Thank you for the invitation, but I can't attend.

- Thank you for asking, but I can't accommodate your request.

- Thank you for giving me time to consider your request, but I can't help you at this time.

- Remember that comment you made earlier about such-and-such? Please don't say things like that again as I felt attacked. Next time, I would appreciate you approaching me with respect and consideration for my feelings.

- Remember when you said such-and-such? I felt insulted/hurt/embarrassed when you said that. Next time, can you please address me in private more respectfully and more constructively?

- Remember the plan you mentioned earlier? I'd really like to do x, y and z instead of a, b and c. What do you think of that?

Learning to express your needs with confidence is a process that takes time and practice. However, it's a skill that will help you gain respect for yourself and improve your communication with others. Which in turn will help other people respect you more and treat you better.

Daily Challenge for Week Five:

Speak Up for Yourself Each Day

Practice delaying answers and responses so you can work on your communication skills. Look for opportunities to delay answering, even if you already know the answer, just to give yourself practice with the three-step process.

If you feel you'd like to address your public speaking ability during this week, consider attending a Toastmasters meeting in your area (or other public groups or seminars if that's not available). You'll get to watch other people speak and learn from their experiences. If you decide to join the group, you'll get to practice public speaking on an ongoing basis.

If you're open to alternative therapies, you may also be interested in methods designed to open your throat chakra. (Your throat chakra is an energy center believed to affect your ability to express yourself confidently.) You may be interested in checking into yoga routines tailored to open the chakras, and activities such as humming, singing, and chanting.

By week five you will:

- Record three things you like about yourself every day.
- Track what occurs on bad days in your Cognitive Behavior Therapy Chart.
- Begin establishing a social support network.
- Write out the answers to the questions in the exercise, and identify changes you'd like to make to honor your true self.
- Record your experiences of speaking up for yourself in your journal.

Facing Your Fears

Overcoming fear of failure can greatly improve your self-confidence. Sound simple enough? Believe it or not it really is that easy. But the real challenge is in identifying and conquering the fear before you can move forward.

Fears range from not doing well enough on the job, to appearing stupid while speaking, or not being savvy enough to make a deal. The trick is to identify what issues are causing the most anxiety, and then ticking off those fears one-by-one to make them disappear and regain control.

The Anxiety Meter

In order to identify the areas of your life that cause you the most trouble, you'll need to identify what tasks or experiences make you the most anxious. To do this you'll need to record your levels of anxiety (on a scale of 1 to 10, with 10 being the most anxious and 1 being the least):

- Late to meeting – anxiety level 3
- Presentation – anxiety level 8
- Meeting with the boss – anxiety level 5
- Dinner party – anxiety level 7

Make a list of things that make you feel anxious during the week. Star the experiences that make you the most anxious as the ones you need to conquer the quickest. Use this list to identify experiences that challenge your confidence level, and then tackle them one-by-one to seriously reduce your levels of anxiety and how it controls the quality of your life.

Anxiety and Modern Medicine: Can a Pill Solve Your Problems?

If anxiety and confidence are linked, shouldn't an anti-anxiety drug help you feel more confident? The answer is maybe yes and maybe no.

Many people swear by anti-anxiety drugs; in fact, 43% of Americans take mood-altering prescriptions drugs every day. Of the prescription drugs taken for anxiety, Paxil and Zoloft have come in as the seventh and eighth most commonly prescribed medications (please consult your physician as the FDA issued a warning in 2009 about Paxil causing serious depression and could possibly trigger suicide and other issues).

One of the biggest concerns regarding anti-anxiety drugs is the side effects. Because anti-anxiety drugs work by slowing mental functions, you may not feel like yourself while on the medication. While you might experience temporary relief from anxiety, the side effects may cause you great distress in other areas. Common side effects are: Addiction, drowsiness, depression, memory loss, mental slowness, lack of motivation.

You should talk to your doctor about trying an anti-anxiety drug if you have crippling anxiety that can't be controlled with therapy or natural remedies. Although some people find anti-anxiety medications to be very effective, it's important to remember that they temporarily relieve symptoms, and usually need to be coupled with therapy or counseling to produce satisfactory long-term results.

Natural Ways to Overcome Anxiety

There are many ways to overcome anxiety as you tackle the issues that cause you the most worries. You might consider the following practices:

- Tackle the problem multiple times. The more often a fear is faced and survived, the less power it has. Mental and emotional expectations surrounding the experience tell you to stop feeling anxious (after all, you made it through the last time you encountered the problem). Create a repetitive, safe way to tackle your fear, and force yourself to overcome it until it feels less stressful.

- Hypnosis cuts past the conscious mind to speak to the subconscious where intellect can't censor the message. Some options include self, group, and individual hypnosis therapy.

- Just 15 minutes of meditation per day can help you overcome anxiety. Sit in a comfortable position in a quiet room, set an alarm, and close your eyes. Focus on your breathing and a simple one-line mantra such as "I can present material to groups", "I am a good speaker", or "I am strong enough." Repeat your mantra as you focus on your breathing, and feel the anxiety leave your body.

All of these practices are natural without unnatural stimulation, and can help you overcome anxiety related to a particular experience.

Daily Challenge for Week Six:

Conquer Your Fear of Failure

Use the anxiety meter to identify a challenge; choose a fear you know you can overcome, then face that fear and overcome it. Don't tackle the most intimidating fear at first; instead tackle something easy. Build your way up to tackling the worst of your fears over time, and record your efforts in your journal.

If you decide that some fears are insurmountable, at some point you may have to ask yourself if it's worth it to keep that experience in your life. If you hate public speaking but have to give presentations at work, you may want to approach your boss and ask if you can be excused from that responsibility and take on another, less stressful task.

Or if you realize big parties stress you out due to social overload, stop going to them. Compartmentalize your social engagements by meeting people for coffee one-on-one, going to the movies, or having couples over for dinner.

Your challenge this week is to identify some of your fears, and to tackle and overcome one small, tiny fear. If you get anxious when you have to introduce yourself in a large meeting, practice your greeting at home in the mirror ahead of time. Then introduce yourself first at a meeting this week. Smile confidently, and speak firmly and clearly.

Compliment yourself when you've finished, and reassure yourself that you no longer fear that issue. Eventually you'll let go of that worry, and you'll be ready to tackle bigger ones.

By week six you will:

- Record three things you like about yourself every day.
- Track what occurs on bad days in your Cognitive Behavior Therapy Chart.
- Begin establishing a social support network.
- Write out the answers to the questions in the exercise, and identify changes you'd like to make to honor your true self.
- Record your experiences of speaking up for yourself in your journal.
- Identify and conquer one or more of your fears.

Get Physical

You might wonder how physical exercise could possibly be related to improving your self-confidence, but it is. Your posture, how you feel about yourself physically, and how you handle stress all affect your self-confidence.

Improve Your Posture

People assess you before you even speak your first words. Are you standing straight? Are your shoulders back or hunched? Does your stance seem forced or relaxed? Body language speaks louder than words by telling how people feel about themselves and how they want to be treated.

Look at yourself in the mirror and relax into your natural stance. Now stand tall, roll your shoulders back, and allow your hands to rest at your sides in a comfortable position. Do you see the difference in attitude you're projecting?

Believe it or not, you will feel more self-assured if you improve your posture. Scientists aren't quite sure if this is because you project a more confident stance (which other people pick up and project back to you, thereby increasing your confidence). Or if this is a physiological response;

simply meaning you'll feel more confident if you stand or sit in a confident pose. In either instance, studies show that improving your posture will result in more self-confidence.

Richard Petty, a professor of psychology at Ohio State University, conducted a study on the link between posture and self-confidence. He had 71 students slump at their desks while writing how and why they qualified for a job opportunity. Later he had them sit straight while answering more questions. Interestingly, the students felt more confident about the words they wrote when they were sitting straight, than the words they wrote when slumped over.

Professor Petty's studies of the connection between body language and confidence supported the concept that how a person holds their body affects (and reflects) how they feel about themselves.

You can improve your posture and body language by working on your core muscles (which are the muscles in your abdomen and back). If you do the following Superman exercise and bicycle crunches each day, you'll find it easier to sit straight, hold your shoulders back, and stand in a proper position that commands respect.

Bicycle Crunches

Lie on your back on a mat or carpeted floor. Support your head by lacing your hands behind your head, and lift your knees to a 90-degree angle. Contracting your oblique muscles and abdominal muscles, pull one of your knees towards the opposing elbow, and twist across your upper body. Now retract the knee and elbow, and bring the other knee to your other elbow as if you are riding a bike. This move works the abdominal, oblique muscles and back muscles all at once. Perform bicycle crunches until you feel the burn, then stretch out on the floor to rest for a few moments. Repeat for three sets.

The Superman Exercise

Lie on your stomach and gently lift up an opposing leg and arm (i.e., left arm and right leg) until you engage the muscles of your lower back. This is a small move, so don't push it. Lower the leg and arm to the ground, then lift the opposite leg and arm, again very carefully. If you feel strong you can lift both arms and legs at the same time to make it look as if you're flying just like Superman. This small move is one of the best exercises to strengthen your lower back muscles.

Walk

Walking is magical when it comes to confidence as it can make you feel strong, healthy, and fit. And when you feel healthy, you're less likely to criticize yourself about your weaknesses.

Walking will improve your confidence because it will accomplish the following:

- You will feel good about yourself because you will have prioritized exercise every day.

- You'll feel more relaxed and able to handle stress (walking naturally releases stress and anxiety).

- It will make you feel happier, and happier people tend to feel more confident.

- It will make you feel stronger and more fit, which boosts confidence.

- By walking every day you'll start to think of yourself as an "exerciser," which will boost positive feelings about yourself since "exercising" is usually associated with "healthy, attractive, and strong" – all of which are positive attributes.

If you already exercise regularly, return to a previous chapter and give yourself an extra week to work on that subject.

Daily Challenge for Week Seven:

Work on Your Posture and Overall Fitness

Every day this week walk for at least 30 minutes; do at least one set of bicycle crunches and the Superman exercise. Be constantly aware of sitting straight and engage your core muscles, and standing straight and rolling back your shoulders.

By week seven you will:

- Record three things you like about yourself every day.

- Track what occurs on bad days in your Cognitive Behavior Therapy Chart.

- Begin establishing a social support network.

- Write out the answers to the questions in the exercise, and identify changes you'd like to make to honor your true self.

- Record your experiences of speaking up for yourself in your journal.

- Identify and conquer one of your fears.

- Establish a weekly routine of improving your posture and overall health.

Intimacy

Intimate relationships play an important part in a person's self-image. When tangible support is received from a friendship or romantic relationship, their confidence soars. Going without physical intimacy or tangible support from close friends starves people emotionally. And one of the first places this starvation reveals itself is in a decrease of self-confidence.

The Psychology of Intimacy and Confidence

Intimate relationships affirm self-worth. Close relationships tell people they are worthy, and that they are good people who deserve to be loved and cherished. Physical expressions of love – especially when delivered by people they respect – make them feel good about themselves. In turn, those good feelings increase self-confidence and the ability to deflect experiences that make people doubt themselves.

A physiological occurrence happens when you get hugged, touched, or held by a friend or romantic partner. If you hug someone for 20 seconds or longer, your body produces a chemical called oxytocin. Oxytocin (a human hormone) makes you feel bonded to that person, so the chemical reaction in your body actually produces an emotional response. That bonding feeling makes you feel as if you belong, which in turn makes you feel safe. And what do you feel when you feel safe? You feel confident.

Daily Challenge for Week Eight:

Hug Someone Every Day

If possible, hug several people during the week, or hug the same person several times. Try to make the hugs last several seconds or longer. Other ideas for the week are:

- Cuddle with someone special (a child or grandchild is a good candidate for this if you don't have a romantic partner) while watching television or a movie.
- Make love with a romantic partner.
- Give and receive a back or foot rub from a friend or partner.

By week eight you will:

- Record three things you like about yourself every day.
- Track what occurs on bad days in your Cognitive Behavior Therapy Chart.
- Begin establishing a social support network.
- Write out the answers to the questions in the exercise, and identify changes you'd like to make to honor your true self.
- Record your experiences of speaking up for yourself in your journal.
- Identify and conquer one of your fears.
- Establish a weekly routine of improving your posture and overall health.
- Hug someone every day.

Imagine

Imagine meeting yourself for the first time. Who is this person? What do you like about them? What things make you want to spend time with them? What things make them unique and interesting? What things make you want to know them better?

Have you ever seen photos of yourself that made you think, *Wow! I look better than I thought*? (Forget about unflattering photos as they belong in the trashcan.) The mind is a powerful tool. If you fill your mind with a positive mental image of yourself, you will feel more confident without even trying.

A study published in the *Journal of Sports Sciences* in 2008 popularized the power of imagery; that is, the practice of imagining yourself succeeding at a task. The study evaluated soccer players who visualized themselves as successful athletes performing sports-related tasks, and compared them to other players who did not engage in any specific imagery practice. The players who practiced positive imagery reported feeling between 40% and 57%

more confident and were able to perform at a higher level of play.

This week you're going to create a visual depiction of the collection of positive attributes you've unearthed about yourself thus far in the program.

Daily Challenge for Week Nine:

Make a Collage Depicting Your Best Self

You'll need a poster board, glue and scissors. Now re-read the many positive things you've listed about yourself in your journal and turn them into a list.

Use pictures from magazines, printouts from the internet, and personal photographs to create a collage representing the things you like best about yourself. Add symbols and totems as you find them through out the week. Finally, add words from your list of things you like about yourself.

By week nine you will:

- Record three things you like about yourself every day.

- Track what occurs on bad days in your Cognitive Behavior Therapy Chart.

- Begin establishing a social support network.

- Write out the answers to the questions in the exercise, and identify changes you'd like to make to honor your true self.

- Record your experiences of speaking up for yourself in your journal.
- Identify and conquer one of your fears.
- Establish a weekly routine of improving your posture and overall health.
- Hug someone every day.
- Add things to each day to your "best you" collage.

Just Do It

There's something extremely fulfilling about learning a new skill or tackling a challenge. Do you remember how you felt on a first day of school, or used a power tool for the first time? Remember how it felt to get behind the wheel of a car with the driver's ed teacher? Or how you felt getting ready for your first job?

Whenever people use their minds and bodies to do something new and challenging, they often experience an elevation in positive feelings. Learning something new improves and reasserts a person's ability to learn, grow, conquer their lack of self-esteem and rediscover their abilities.

Even thought the very act of trying something new – which can be intimidating – can push people to be brave and strong, the fear of the unknown can keep them stuck where they feel safe and comfortable.

But taking on new challenges forces people out of their ruts. When life gets too familiar they can get bored, and in turn boredom leads to discouragement and negativity.

Daily Challenge for Week Ten:

Identify and Commit to Accomplishing a Personal Goal

Have you dreamt of opening your own business or freelancing instead of working in an office? Have you fantasized about running a half marathon or patenting an invention? Have you wanted to learn a foreign language or travel to another country? Have you longed to experiment with investments or sell some of your artwork?

If any of these possibilities have resonated with you, now is the time to set your goals in motion. Use this week to make plans to actualize your dreams. Invest time in learning something new or accomplishing something you find exciting. You may want to:

- Join a group
- Sign up for a class
- Go to a local Meet Up or networking meeting
- Buy an educational book
- Enroll in an online course
- Register a patent or invention
- Write out a business plan
- Buy a plane ticket

By week ten you will:

- Record three things you like about yourself every day.

- Track what occurs on bad days in your Cognitive Behavior Therapy Chart.

- Begin establishing a social support network.

- Write out the answers to the questions in the exercise, and identify changes you'd like to make to honor your true self.

- Record your experiences of speaking up for yourself in your journal.

- Identify and conquer one of your fears.

- Establish a weekly routine of improving your posture and overall health.

- Hug someone every day.

- Add things to each day to your "best you" collage.

- Start planning to actualize at least one of your dreams.

Keep Looking for Ways to Help

The legendary Zig Ziglar said, "You can get anything in life you want if you help enough other people get what they want." That goes double when talking about boosting self-confidence.

When you help someone who doesn't understand something, or feels weak when you feel strong, you would normally feel a natural sense of pride. Doing something good makes you aware that you are a strong, competent individual.

The Link Between Altruism and Confidence

According to psychologist Daniel Batson, author of *The Altruism Question*, altruistic acts improve feelings of self-worth. As people perform benevolent acts they see themselves as caring, capable, generous, and considerate. In other words, altruistic acts help people build self-confidence while strengthening and protecting their self-esteem.

Daily Challenge for Week 11:

Help Someone Every Day

Look for opportunities to help someone every day. Some possibilities are:

- A co-worker who is less competent than you.
- A neighbor or relative who is less mechanically inclined, technically savvy, or physically not as strong as you.
- A child who needs tutoring or help with homework.
- Someone who is physically or mentally disabled
- An animal in need of help.

This is a good time to consider volunteering for a charitable organization. You may find rewarding opportunities through some of the following examples:

- Assisting teachers or tutoring opportunities
- A local church or synagogue
- Local Humane Society or other animal rescue group
- Habitat for Humanity
- Red Cross
- Homeless shelters or hospices
- Big Brother/Big Sister Organizations

By week 11 you will:

- Record three things you like about yourself every day.

- Track what occurs on bad days in your Cognitive Behavior Therapy Chart.

- Begin establishing a social support network.

- Write out the answers to the questions in the exercise, and identify changes you'd like to make to honor your true self.

- Record your experiences of speaking up for yourself in your journal.

- Identify and conquer one of your fears.

- Establish a weekly routine of improving your posture and overall health.

- Hug someone every day.

- Add things to each day to your "best you" collage.

- Start planning to actualize at least one of your dreams.

- Find ways to help others through volunteering and humanitarian efforts. Record how you feel about your efforts.

Week 12

Laugh at Yourself

What do you think is the most defining attribute of a confident person? Is it that they're better than everyone else? Is it that they're more competent or better looking than everyone else?

The most common trait of confident people is that they don't take themselves too seriously and can laugh at themselves.

People who lack confidence tend to possess characteristics psychologists like David Burns (author of *Feeling Good*) call "cognitive distortions." That is, they take an experience and distort it in their mind.

Cognitive distortions may show up as:

- All or nothing thinking: Where falling short is seen as a total failure instead of a momentary setback.
- Mental filter: When something bad happens, a person can only think about the negative and cannot find anything positive.
- Magnification: Exaggerating anything bad that happened.

- Minimizing: Downplaying or discounting anything good that happened.

- Narcissism: When a tiny mistake is seen as big enough to warrant the attention of others, when in reality nobody is probably thinking about it.

Learning to Combat Cognitive Distortions

If you tend to fall prey to cognitive distortions (see above), you're probably very hard on yourself if you feel less than perfect. This tendency to punish yourself for failure can erode your sense of adventure and joy for life. In addition, holding back instead of risking failure can cripple you emotionally.

You can, however, combat cognitive distortions by using two very powerful weapons: Humor and Grace.

The Power of Humor

When something goes wrong and you find yourself sliding into a distortion of the facts, stop and look for something humorous about the situation. Laughing off a mistake will accomplish the following:

- You'll bond with whomever is present, since laughter brings people together.

- You'll deflate the situation and prevent it from being magnified in your mind.

- You'll open yourself to other solutions, since the very act of laughing at the problem will minimize it. This will help overcome the tendency to fall into an all-or-nothing mindset.

- Open yourself to encouragement from others
  (people tend to reassure those who make jokes at
  their own expense).

All of these possibilities will help switch your thinking
from negative to positive, and help protect your self-esteem.

The Power of Grace

If you can't laugh at yourself, you should at least forgive
yourself. This might sound simplistic, but it's scientifically
proven that if you switch from thinking about yourself in
first person to third person, you can forgive yourself faster
and move on from your mistakes.

Thomas Gilovich, professor of psychology at Cornell,
teamed up with assistant professors Lisa Libby (Ohio State
University) and Richard Eibach (Yale University) to study
the effect of retelling memories in third person.

The study concluded that people were more solution-
oriented and more likely to make positive changes when
they thought about themselves in third person as opposed
to first person. Which means that forgiving yourself (in
third person) maybe exactly the extra boost you need to
move on and let go of regret and shame.

When trying to forgive yourself you can follow these
steps mentally, out loud, or written in your journal:

- Put the mistake in perspective.
- Ask yourself who the mistake affected.

- Make amends where possible.
- Remind yourself of your good intentions.
- Look for reasons why you made the mistake, and promise yourself to learn from the experience.
- Actively forgive yourself.
- Take action to remedy the situation, make amends, or move on to something positive if there is nothing else that can be done.

Forgiving yourself will help you handle the situation with grace and self-respect. Feeling good about how you handled the mistake will help you feel better about yourself.

Daily Challenge for Week 12:

Work on Your Sense of Humor

Try making fun of yourself the next time you make a mistake. If this doesn't suit your personality, try forgiving yourself. Examine the mistake, put it in perspective, and tell yourself it's okay. (How much of an impact did it make? How likely is it that anyone remembers it? Would you care if someone else made the same mistake?) If you find this difficult, you can pretend you're talking to another person (some people are better at forgiving others than themselves).

As you go through the week to increase your grace and sense of humor, watch for mistakes other people make and ask yourself was it really all that bad? Am I able to laugh at their mistake or forgive them? Soon you will realize how laughter and grace makes the world a better place.

By week 12 you will:

- Record three things you like about yourself every day.

- Track what occurs on bad days in your Cognitive Behavior Therapy Chart.

- Begin establishing a social support network.

- Write out the answers to the questions in the exercise, and identify changes you'd like to make to honor your true self.

- Record your experiences of speaking up for yourself in your journal.

- Identify and conquer one of your fears.

- Establish a weekly routine of improving your posture and overall health.

- Hug someone every day.

- Add things to each day to your "best you" collage.

- Start planning to actualize at least one of your dreams.

- Find ways to help others through volunteering and humanitarian efforts. Record how you feel about your efforts.

- Add humor and grace to your list of positive attributes.

Marvel at Your Accomplishments

People tend to focus more on their failures than their accomplishments. Some parents downplay their children's accomplishments because they fear they will become cocky and over-confident. If you tend to think more about failures than victories, this chapter is for you.

How Do You Tell Your Life Story?

When you think of your life thus far, do you feel satisfied or discouraged? When someone asks you to describe yourself, do you emphasize the positive or the negative?

Why is it that some people who have endured terrible trauma and setbacks exude confidence and optimism? Why is it that others who have had every privilege are negative and insecure? The key is how they recall their life stories.

People who have endured trauma and view themselves as "survivors" and "heroes" tend to be positive and confident. People born with silver spoons in their mouths, but view themselves as "victims," are often insecure and negative.

Putting a positive spin on your life's experiences can make you a more confident, much better person.

Why Your Life Story Matters: Understanding Personal Narratives

Narrative therapy is an advanced trend in psychotherapy that entails revising the way a person tells their life story. Memories are imperfect, which makes it possible to positively or negatively skew stories as they are remembered and presented to others.

When remembering events from the past people often:

- Exaggerate
- Minimize
- Generalize
- Forget events altogether
- Focus on a few select experiences

Such deficits can significantly sabotage your overall view of yourself, which is why it's important to periodically review your history to get the facts straight.

While reviewing your narrative you can diminish events that eroded your self-esteem, and remember events that made you feel stronger and more confident. You'll improve your overall outlook, and view future events in a more confident and positive light.

Daily Challenge for Week 13:

Make a List of Accomplishments and Achievements

Go through your history year-by-year, and write down every accomplishment or achievement you can remember. Take your time to reflect on as much of your past as possible, and allow this exercise to consume your entire week. If you finish the list before the week is over, choose your favorite life accomplishment and write it out in story form as a personal narrative.

By week 13 you will:

- Record three things you like about yourself every day.
- Track what occurs on bad days in your Cognitive Behavior Therapy Chart.
- Begin establishing a social support network.
- Write out the answers to the questions in the exercise, and identify changes you'd like to make to honor your true self.
- Record your experiences of speaking up for yourself in your journal.
- Identify and conquer one of your fears.
- Establish a weekly routine of improving your posture and overall health.
- Hug someone every day.
- Add things to each day to your "best you" collage.

- Start planning to actualize at least one of your dreams.

- Find ways to help others through volunteering and humanitarian efforts. Record how you feel about your efforts.

- Add humor and grace to your list of positive attributes.

- Set down your personal narrative of accomplishments and achievements to journal your life's history.

Nurture Yourself

If you struggle with self-confidence, there's a good chance you're dealing with high levels of stress. As discussed earlier, anxiety and insecurity are greatly intertwined; therefore, many people with poor self-esteem or self-confidence experience a great deal of anxiety.

This week's lesson addresses dealing with stress and anxiety to prevent emotional battering. Stress and anxiety can assault a person's emotional and physical well-being, and the following symptoms should be seen as red flags:

- Fatigue
- Vulnerability to illness
- Tense muscles
- Upset stomach
- Insomnia
- High blood pressure

When you're stressed, your body produces too much of a hormone called cortisol which is tolerable when in small amounts. But in large doses, cortisol can wear down your general physical health and cause the following health problems:

- Weakened immune system
- Poor cognitive performance (not thinking clearly)
- Blood sugar problems (increased risk of diabetes)
- Increase in accumulation of abdominal fat
- Impaired muscle tissue repair

As you can see, it's important to learn how to manage the high stress that accompanies low self-confidence.

Prioritize Proper Self-Care

Prioritizing your well-being is not only an act of self-love, but a way to prove that you're worth the time and energy you invest in self-care.

The following are suggestions for self-care that will reduce your stress and cortisol levels, and increase your self-love:

- Meditation
- Yoga
- Massage
- Gentle exercise (running, walking) and stretching
- Pedicure, manicure, facials
- Getting your hair cut and styled
- Reading a book, watching a movie, listening to music
- Taking a long bath

- Reflexology (foot massage)
- Reiki (energy healing)

Daily Challenge for Week 14:
Take Time to De-stress

Find ways to take care of yourself every day this week. You might treat yourself to a glass of wine and a long bath one night, and go for a languorous hike the next day. Find some way to unwind and take care of yourself each day, remembering that a good defense is as effective as a good offense.

By week 14 you will:

- Record three things you like about yourself every day.
- Track what occurs on bad days in your Cognitive Behavior Therapy Chart.
- Begin establishing a social support network.
- Write out the answers to the questions in the exercise, and identify changes you'd like to make to honor your true self.
- Record your experiences of speaking up for yourself in your journal.
- Identify and conquer one of your fears.
- Establish a weekly routine of improving your posture and overall health.

- Hug someone every day.
- Add things to each day to your "best you" collage.
- Start planning to actualize at least one of your dreams.
- Find ways to help others through volunteering and humanitarian efforts. Record how you feel about your efforts.
- Add humor and grace to your list of positive attributes.
- Set down your personal narrative of accomplishments and achievements to journal your life's history.
- Take time to nurture yourself.

Romance

Perhaps one of the most obvious ways confidence affects people is in their romantic relationships.

Studies have shown that negative emotions can lead to poor partner choice and a lower ability to weather the ups and downs of a relationship. According to relationship self-help guru Liv Miyagawa, addressing self-confidence issues can help you choose better romantic partners who will treat you lovingly and with respect.

This week you're going to examine the ways your confidence affects your romantic relationships, even if you aren't in a romantic relationship at the moment.

Your Confidence Level and Romantic Past

Earlier you were asked to retell your life history by focusing on events and experiences that made you feel good about yourself. This week you're going to evaluate how your confidence level in the past has affected your romantic relationships, and take steps towards improving your chances for more positive unions.

Without dwelling on this topic too long you should try to answer the following questions:

- Am I pleased with the quality of the partners I have chosen?

- Have my partners treated me with dignity and respect?

- When I look at my current romantic prospects or relationship, do I feel admired, respected, and cherished?

- What would I like to do differently in my romantic relationships going forward?

Common Areas to Address

As you're reviewing your romantic history, you may realize you:

- Chose partners who were not as respectful or loving as you deserved.

- Gave up on relationships too soon because you assumed things would go wrong (which they usually did).

- Did not initiate or give relationships a chance out of self-protection.

- Have kept your romantic partner at an emotional distance because you fear getting hurt or judgment for your emotions.

You can probably blame your lack of confidence if you identified with any of the above. The good news is you can choose to behave differently in the future:

- Only date or live with a partner who is respectful and loving.

- Ask your current partner to treat you in a respectful and loving manner.

- Persevere with a current partner if you believe the two of you can work things out.

- Initiate romance with a desired partner, and take a chance on love (realizing that if you are turned down you still value your self-worth).

- Open up to your current romantic partner to build a deeper, more satisfying relationship

Satisfying romantic relationships build our self-esteem and can become significant parts of our emotional foundation. If this is an area of concern for you, this might be the right time for you to seek help from a relationship counselor or therapist. Choose love and support as it's very – VERY – good for your emotional health.

Daily Challenge for Week 15:

Evaluate and Improve Your Romantic Relationships

Use this week to:

- Initiate a new romantic relationship (ask someone out, check out an online dating service, invest time in a friendship you'd like to see advance romantically).

- Ask for more love or respect from a current romantic relationship.

- Open yourself up to a more intimate relationship.

- Heal wounds from past romantic relationships.

You may wish to do this with the support of a friend, therapist, or your trusty journal (sometimes you are your best support system). As you make progress, remind yourself of the many reasons why you deserve to be loved, respected and cherished.

By week 15 you will:

- Record three things you like about yourself every day.

- Track what occurs on bad days in your Cognitive Behavior Therapy Chart.

- Begin establishing a social support network.

- Write out the answers to the questions in the exercise, and identify changes you'd like to make to honor your true self.

- Record your experiences of speaking up for yourself in your journal.

- Identify and conquer one of your fears.

- Establish a weekly routine of improving your posture and overall health.

- Hug someone every day.

- Add things to each day to your "best you" collage.

- Start planning to actualize at least one of your dreams.

- Find ways to help others through volunteering and humanitarian efforts. Record how you feel about your efforts.

- Add humor and grace to your list of positive attributes.

- Set down your personal narrative of accomplishments and achievements to journal your life's history.

- Take time to nurture yourself.

- Open yourself to new romantic relationships and heal old wounds.

Pave the Way

Have you ever led a project at work? Headed a committee in your community? Gotten the top score in class, or finished a project ahead of schedule and under budget?

Performance is inherently linked to confidence, since people feel good when they perform at or above their expectations. A surge of positive emotions is felt whenever goals are met or a group is led to victory. This is why parents of insecure children often send them away to Girl or Boy Scout camps, or to put them in sports to learn how to successfully lead their teams. The very act of risk-taking can be very powerful.

Your current circumstances may not allow you to experience achievement or leadership on a regular basis. Perhaps you're a member of a team, but not the team leader. Maybe you've been assigned to a project, but not the project manager as you're the youngest person or take the longest to complete tasks.

Fortunately, you can control several of your life circumstances (meaning you can lead the way to victory, even if your workplace hasn't set you up to do so). This week you're going to take risks, and savor the sense of accomplishment associated with success.

Daily Challenge for Week 16:

Find Ways to Lead and Succeed

This week you're going to look for opportunities to be a leader. Consider the following suggestions:

- Lead a project for your child, grandchild or neighbor's Girl Scout or Boy Scout Troop by capitalizing on your strengths. You could lead the children on hikes, teach them how to build a fire or about nutrition, or lead a class on crafts – whatever suits your particular skills.

- Volunteer to handle a tough assignment at work and then knock it out of the park.

- Use your expertise to train someone less experienced. This could mean training volunteers at the Humane Society, teaching someone how to use a computer, or mentoring a young artist.

- Offer to sponsor someone through AA or NA.

- Help an elderly neighbor with a task they shouldn't be doing on their own.

- Offer to lead a group at your church or community organizations.

- Join the PTA or PTO and offer to organize a fundraising event.

By week 16 you will:

- Record three things you like about yourself every day.

- Track what occurs on bad days in your Cognitive Behavior Therapy Chart.

- Begin establishing a social support network.

- Write out the answers to the questions in the exercise, and identify changes you'd like to make to honor your true self.

- Record your experiences of speaking up for yourself in your journal.

- Identify and conquer one of your fears.

- Establish a weekly routine of improving your posture and overall health.

- Hug someone every day.

- Add things to each day to your "best you" collage.

- Start planning to actualize at least one of your dreams.

- Find ways to help others through volunteering and humanitarian efforts. Record how you feel about your efforts.

- Add humor and grace to your list of positive attributes.

- Set down your personal narrative of accomplishments and achievements to journal your life's history.

- Take time to nurture yourself.

- Open yourself to new romantic relationships and heal old wounds.

- Look for ways to lead people and events to success.

Reset Boundaries

Building self-confidence entails a combination of various efforts. In this section you're going to discover a way to protect yourself from people who bully you.

You've probably encountered critical people who knock you down or pick on you (subtly or not so subtly), and have negatively affected your confidence. Some people criticize openly, but others criticize in behavior disguised to look innocent or acceptable. For example, a friend or partner who asks "Why did you do that?" or "Why did you do that this way?" is subliminally insinuating that you made a bad choice and need to justify your actions.

Another critical communication is when a person starts sentences with, "What you really need to do is…" or "You should really do…" This type of statement insinuates that you can't figure things out on your own and need guidance so you won't make mistakes. Such negative statements undermine your faith in yourself since it puts you on the defensive and creates self-doubt.

Identify Negative People

You may think, *I know who the negative people in my life are*, and maybe you do. However, most people adapt to the way they're treated, and may be unaware that negative energy is affecting their self-esteem.

Think about your friends and co-workers, and evaluate how positive or negative they come across when interacting with you. Ask yourself the following questions, and then rank each person on a scale of one to ten (one being unsupportive and highly critical; ten being very supportive and not critical at all):

- Do they support me and my efforts?
- Do they criticize me often? Is the criticism constructive or destructive? Does this person help me succeed or discourage me?
- Do they compliment me and build me up?
- Do they tell me what I should do and try to control me?
- How do I feel after interacting with this person?
- Do I look forward to interacting with them, or try to avoid them?

Once you've rated the people in your life, consider what you can do to limit or eliminate your interactions with people who rank below a five. Then ask yourself the following questions:

- Do I have to interact with this person, or should I cut them out altogether?

- How much do I have to interact with them?
- Are there creative ways I could limit contact with them?
- If I have to interact with this negative individual, how can I address the issues at hand?
- Can I set boundaries as to how they are allowed to contact or interact with me?
- Should I ask them to interact with me in a more positive way? If so, what is a socially acceptable way to set new boundaries?

After you have answered these questions, set new boundaries or limit interactions with as many negative people as possible.

Daily Challenge for Week 17:

Set Boundaries to Protect Yourself

Spend one day evaluating your relationships with friends and co-workers. Once you've determined who the negative influences are, decide how you want to limit interactions or set new boundaries. Make it a goal to accomplish this by the end of the week.

By week 17 you will:

- Record three things you like about yourself every day.
- Track what occurs on bad days in your Cognitive Behavior Therapy Chart.

- Begin establishing a social support network.
- Write out the answers to the questions in the exercise, and identify changes you'd like to make to honor your true self.
- Record your experiences of speaking up for yourself in your journal.
- Identify and conquer one of your fears.
- Establish a weekly routine of improving your posture and overall health.
- Hug someone every day.
- Add things to each day to your "best you" collage.
- Start planning to actualize at least one of your dreams.
- Find ways to help others through volunteering and humanitarian efforts. Record how you feel about your efforts.
- Add humor and grace to your list of positive attributes.
- Set down your personal narrative of accomplishments and achievements to journal your life's history.
- Take time to nurture yourself.
- Open yourself to new romantic relationships and heal old wounds.
- Look for ways to lead people and events to success.
- Eliminate negative people from your life, and establish boundaries of protection.

Star in Your Own Show

While everyone has unique talents, it's easy to allow others to give value to your skill sets. This week you're going to ignore people's need to judge, and instead be your own critic as your explore and use talents unique to you.

Self-confidence is based on the belief that you have something unique to offer. When you understand that your unusual flavor is appreciated you'll grow in your "star appeal." It doesn't matter if your audience is large or small; the only thing that matters is that you discover the true value of your talents.

Discovering Your Talent

What if you don't think you have talent? You may have gotten so busy with work, family, and obligations that you've forgotten what your talents are. Or you may have hidden them due to the negative reactions of people around you.

Many people benefit from revisiting their childhood interests where their desires and talents were first sprouted. What did you like to do as a ten-year-old child? As a preschooler or teenager? What aspirations did you have for your life before you knew about limitations (such as salaries)? What topics now catch your eye when you scan magazines or news articles, or watch television?

Consider the following possible areas of talent as you look for your unique way to contribute to the world.

Visual Art

Can you paint, sketch, sculpt or create mixed media? Try creating works of your own, then approach a local gallery about submitting your favorite pieces. Mat, frame and hang your artwork, or give it as gifts. Consider renting a booth at an art fair to showcase your work.

Physical Strength

If you enjoy using your body you might consider helping a friend move, volunteering at a boxing ring, or other physical labor. Maybe you have a neighbor who needs help with a labor-intensive job.

Mechanical Handiness

If fixing broken things appeals to you, consider advertising your skills online (i.e., angieslist.com) and periodically taking on clients.

Outdoor Skills

Do you like to camp, hike, and do yard work? You might organize a local co-op or community garden, volunteer to do beautification work for a school or community center, or offer to help an elderly neighbor with their yard. You could also volunteer with the Boy or Girl Scouts and organize camping events.

Physical Exercise

If you're happiest when working out, check into biking or running clubs, and community-run sports centers for volunteer opportunities.

Working With Animals

Do you love animals? Check out opportunities with horse ranches, farms and animal rescue groups. Your local zoo probably has a volunteer program where you can show animals to the public or assist employees.

Medical Knowledge

If you enjoy the medical field, consider working with a blood drive or writing blogposts for medical websites.

Musical Talent

Can you sing or play an instrument? Check out karaoke nights in pubs and coffee shops, teach lessons at a music store, or perform in a local choir or theater company.

People Skills

If you're good with people, you might volunteer for a suicide hotline, sit with family members at hospitals, or perform hospice care. Bring meals to shut-ins, assist the unemployed with resumes, or work in a soup kitchen.

Unique Talent

Do you know how to ride a unicycle? Perform magic tricks? Paint graffiti? Look into opportunities to inspire children through unusual talents and wacky stunts.

Sense of Humor

Check out stand-up comedy nights or writing comic strips. You can submit your work to a variety of websites for review and possible exposure.

Daily Challenge for Week 18:

Rediscover Your Talents

Paint a picture, redecorate a room, volunteer in hospice, walk a neighbor's dog. Find something you excel at and love to do, enjoy your time doing it, and make a plan for incorporating this unique talent into your life.

By week 18 you will:

- Record three things you like about yourself every day.

- Track what occurs on bad days in your Cognitive Behavior Therapy Chart.

- Begin establishing a social support network.

- Write out the answers to the questions in the exercise, and identify changes you'd like to make to honor your true self.

- Record your experiences of speaking up for yourself in your journal.

- Identify and conquer one of your fears.

- Establish a weekly routine of improving your posture and overall health.

- Hug someone every day.

- Add things to each day to your "best you" collage.

- Start planning to actualize at least one of your dreams.

- Find ways to help others through volunteering and humanitarian efforts. Record how you feel about your efforts.

- Add humor and grace to your list of positive attributes.

- Set down your personal narrative of accomplishments and achievements to journal your life's history.

- Take time to nurture yourself.

- Open yourself to new romantic relationships and heal old wounds.

- Look for ways to lead people and events to success.

- Eliminate negative people from your life, and establish boundaries of protection.

- Whatever your unique talent is, it's your time to shine! Star in your own private show by using the skills that make you feel good about yourself.

Trust Your Instincts

If you lack confidence, you may find yourself doing one or both of these two things:

1. *Doubting your own judgment, and deferring to others when making decisions.*

2. *Stuck in a state of indecision, unable to make quick decisions.*

While over-confidence can produce poor judgment, lack of confidence is also related to the inability to make good decisions. Deliberating too long, or gathering too many opinions and options can overwhelm you, and the waters can be muddied to the point where the correct answer is no longer clearly visible.

Then, when someone overly-controlling forces you to make a decision when your instincts say otherwise, you can end up giving in to their opinion. The end result is you feel out of control, which leads to more self-doubt and resentment. Unless you learn to rely on your instincts, you can continually fall into the trap of people controlling your choices.

This week you're required to track your decision-making process. Set up a chart in your journal and record decisions that have troubled you. Was it difficult for you to decide whether to speak up in a meeting or keep quiet? Did you agonize over a purchase? Did you struggle with making plans? Did you say you wanted something but gave in to someone else's desire (which left you feeling disappointed and unappreciated)?

Carefully examine why you were afraid of making a wrong decision, explore what the outcomes could have been if you had chosen differently, and record the reasons behind your hesitation.

What would have been so bad about speaking up in the meeting? What's the worst thing that could happen if you make an unwise purchase? What would be so awful about canceling plans when you realize you shouldn't have agreed to go? Who did you allow to influence your decision-making? And how did you feel about their influence over you? Are any of these life and death decisions, or just temporary impositions?

Once you've determined what your decision-making patterns are, consider taking more risks. You may find all that deliberation and hesitation carried a hefty price tag of time and stress, but not much (if at all) in the way of rewards. Trust your gut this week, rely more on your knowledge and instincts, and document any positive or negative outcomes.

Daily Challenge for Week 19:

Make a Decision Without Consulting Anyone Else

This might mean you sell stocks from your portfolio and invest in something you have a hunch about or researched. Or you might decide to take a trip to a new part of the country or a new country altogether. You might do something simple like drive a different route to work each day or cook something new. Or something bolder like asking your boss if you can take on a new project.

Whatever you do, be sure to check in with your instincts and trust your judgment. Take bigger and bigger risks (without harm, of course, to you or anyone) and see how it all turns out.

By week 19 you will:

- Record three things you like about yourself every day.
- Track what occurs on bad days in your Cognitive Behavior Therapy Chart.
- Begin establishing a social support network.
- Write out the answers to the questions in the exercise, and identify changes you'd like to make to honor your true self.
- Record your experiences of speaking up for yourself in your journal.
- Identify and conquer one of your fears.

- Establish a weekly routine of improving your posture and overall health.

- Hug someone every day.

- Add things to each day to your "best you" collage.

- Start planning to actualize at least one of your dreams.

- Find ways to help others through volunteering and humanitarian efforts. Record how you feel about your efforts.

- Add humor and grace to your list of positive attributes.

- Set down your personal narrative of accomplishments and achievements to journal your life's history.

- Take time to nurture yourself.

- Open yourself to new romantic relationships and heal old wounds.

- Look for ways to lead people and events to success.

- Eliminate negative people from your life, and establish boundaries of protection.

- Whatever your unique talent is, it's your time to shine! Star in your own private show by using the skills that make you feel good about yourself.

- Learn to trust your gut instincts by taking risks to eliminate the fear of judgment and losing sight of your choices.

Vanquish Vanities

It's becoming more evident every day that today's society is vain and self-indulgent (vanity services such as plastic surgery – both for men and women – and the diet and technological industries generate billions of dollars of revenue).

According to research published in *The Wesleyan Journal of Psychology,* eating disorders have doubled in the past 40 years. Researcher Sara Cohen reports that media (television, movies, magazines, internet, social networking) have created an unrealistic image of the ideal man and woman. Warped perspectives of what is beautiful – instead of admiring real bodies with all their natural flaws – make people compare their faces, hair, bodies, and apparel to very young and abnormally thin airbrushed models.

As a result, all this vanity has cultivated a society of insecure Americans. *Glamour* magazine, which conducted a survey of its readers, stated that 97% of women have negative thoughts about their body, and the average American woman has 13 "brutal" thoughts about her physique every single day. A quarter of the women surveyed by MSNBC admitted to considering plastic surgery (most will continue to going under the knife).

Men aren't exempt from such cruel aberrations of self-image. They have to deal with judgments about their height, weight, bulk, and general attractiveness (the higher their level of employment, the more stressful the pressure to be perfect and young). For example, taller men make about $789 more per inch of height than shorter men (according to Arianne Cohen who wrote *The Tall Book*).

It doesn't take a rocket scientist to explain how this mega-focus on appearances can destroy a person's self-confidence. However, you might be interested in finding out that even inherently attractive people – the ones the general public rates as attractive – can suffer from poor body image and low self-esteem (which is often why you hear about fashion models starving themselves or overdosing on diet drugs).

On the flip side, inherently unattractive people – the ones the general public rates as unattractive – can see themselves as attractive and have high self-esteem.

So what's the trick? Learning to appreciate your appearance, apart from social comparisons to other people, is the key to feeling good about your self-image, which will carry into all areas of your life.

Learn to Love Your Appearance

Easier said than done, right? The following exercises will help you expand this area of appreciating your appearance and cultivating a healthy body image.

Normalize Your View of Yourself

Take note of how very few people really look like models. Every time you think an unfair thought about your appearance, remind yourself that everyone has the same thoughts – even the people you believe are more attractive than you are – and ease up on your negative self-talk.

Admire Yourself

Make a note of ways you're more attractive than some people. Pay attention to things you like about your face, hair, skin and body. Play up those features, and downplay the things you don't particularly care for.

Widen Your Scope of Beauty

Society tends to place emphasis and value on specific traits (weight, height, curves, muscular definition, etc.). Start noticing traits you like or dislike in people, aside from the conventional standard of what is considered beautiful.

Then think about people's endearing traits. Perhaps you love your best friend's laugh lines at her eyes, or your husband's crooked smile. Maybe the way your daughter's brow furrows when she's doing her homework, or how your spouse's skin feels when you're cuddle in bed at night are attributes you find particularly delightful.

Start a Collection of New Beauty Role Models

Observe people who don't wear make-up, are comfortable with their weight and body shape, and exude confidence and kind spirits. Start a mental gallery of those role models and strive to be one of them.

Daily Challenge for Week 20:

Make Yourself Into a New Beauty Role Model

Add yourself to your new beauty role model gallery. Celebrate your uniqueness and become more comfortable in your own skin. Practice this self-love each day, focus on the things you love about your appearance, and appreciate who you are.

When you start thinking something negative about your appearance, remind yourself that everyone has similar thoughts, and that you should not accept them as true or helpful. Then look at your new role models, and imitate their attitudes towards beauty and self-love.

By week 20 you will:

- Record three things you like about yourself every day.
- Track what occurs on bad days in your Cognitive Behavior Therapy Chart.
- Begin establishing a social support network.
- Write out the answers to the questions in the exercise, and identify changes you'd like to make to honor your true self.
- Record your experiences of speaking up for yourself in your journal.
- Identify and conquer one of your fears.

- Establish a weekly routine of improving your posture and overall health.

- Hug someone every day.

- Add things to each day to your "best you" collage.

- Start planning to actualize at least one of your dreams.

- Find ways to help others through volunteering and humanitarian efforts. Record how you feel about your efforts.

- Add humor and grace to your list of positive attributes.

- Set down your personal narrative of accomplishments and achievements to journal your life's history.

- Take time to nurture yourself.

- Open yourself to new romantic relationships and heal old wounds.

- Look for ways to lead people and events to success.

- Eliminate negative people from your life, and establish boundaries of protection.

- Whatever your unique talent is, it's your time to shine! Star in your own private show by using the skills that make you feel good about yourself.

- Trust your gut instincts by taking risks to eliminate the fear of judgment and losing sight of your choices.

- Build a stronger sense of self-image and learn to love who you are.

Write Your Own Destiny

Today is the first day of the rest of your life. You are in control of who you will be today, the next day, and the day after that. You get to decide how and where you work, where you live, how you speak, and your stature. You and only you get to choose it all!

What will you do with your life? What impacts do you want to make? What legacy do you want to leave? What areas of interest and growth will you choose to focus on?

Sonja Lyubomirsky, author of *The How of Happiness*, observed the links between how people spend their time and how happy and confident they are. She asserts that several studies concluded that people who spend a lot of time thinking instead of are generally less happy than people who actively pursue their goals and leisure time.

So what does that mean for you? It means it's time to take all this information you've learned and formulate a redesigned life plan. During the course of this program you've performed many exercises to help you discover the following:

- Reasons to like who you are.

- What activities make you feel best about yourself.
- What relationships are most beneficial for your self-esteem.
- Ways to recover from discouragement and negative self-talk

Your Life Plan

A life plan is similar to a business plan, only much more fun. Follow these steps to create your life plan based on your newfound knowledge of what things increase your self-confidence and what to avoid if you wish to flourish.

Identify Your Dreams

What changes will make you happiest? What experiences would bring you the most satisfaction? What will make you feel happy and proud of who you are as a person?

Set Goals

What would you like to achieve in the years ahead? Have you set tangible goals? Write down milestones and benchmarks to chart your progress as you pursue those goals.

List Your Resources

What unique talents and strengths do you wish to use? Who would you like to accompany you on your journey? What activities, people or experiences will strengthen your self-confidence and make your dreams come true?

Daily Challenge for Week 21:

Write Your Life Plan

Read through your journal notes and compile the information into logical sections. What exercises helped you the most? What changes have worked best for you? What do you want to emphasize as you move forward with your life?

Summarize this information in a life plan, and review it when you need a reminder of who you are and what you want to do with your life.

By week 21 you will:

- Record three things you like about yourself every day.
- Track what occurs on bad days in your Cognitive Behavior Therapy Chart.
- Begin establishing a social support network.
- Write out the answers to the questions in the exercise, and identify changes you'd like to make to honor your true self.
- Record your experiences of speaking up for yourself in your journal.
- Identify and conquer one of your fears.
- Establish a weekly routine of improving your posture and overall health.
- Hug someone every day.
- Add things to each day to your "best you" collage.

- Start planning to actualize at least one of your dreams.

- Find ways to help others through volunteering and humanitarian efforts. Record how you feel about your efforts.

- Add humor and grace to your list of positive attributes.

- Set down your personal narrative of accomplishments and achievements to journal your life's history.

- Take time to nurture yourself.

- Open yourself to new romantic relationships and heal old wounds.

- Look for ways to lead people and events to success.

- Eliminate negative people from your life, and establish boundaries of protection.

- Whatever your unique talent is, it's your time to shine! Star in your own private show by using the skills that make you feel good about yourself.

- Trust your gut instincts by taking risks to eliminate the fear of judgment and losing sight of your choices.

- Build a stronger sense of self-image and learn to love who you are.

- Set your mission statement in motion to build your destiny.

What to Do Now

Self-confidence doesn't require good looks, a huge salary, or an expensive and impressive set of college degrees. However, self-confidence is dependent upon your ability to identify your potential.

The steps outlined in each chapter are designed to help you create your own confidence and better self-image. While it's unlikely that you will continue to practice all 21 principles every day (although it would be a terrific habit to acquire), it is hoped that you've identified which of these exercises work best for you.

As time passes many of these principles will naturally elevate your confidence level as they will have become ingrained as personality traits.

The legendary Benjamin Franklin chose 13 character traits he wanted to master. Each week he would focus on a different attribute, and once the 13 weeks were completed he started over. He worked on this plan every day for more than 50 years, and looking at his accomplishments proves that his plan worked. It will work for you too if you apply the principles in this guide to your life.

It's our wish that you use these steps to learn how to overcome shyness, feel great about who you are, and become more outgoing and confident. Starting taking action today, and you'll be amazed at your newfound ability to meet people, present ideas, and be a leader as you step into the world with confidence!

* * *

For a free book of Napoleon Hill's classic
Think and Grow Rich, **go to:**

www.Get-My-Free-Book.net

* * *

Other eBooks from Laurenzana Press

The Strangest Secret by Earl Nightingale

Memory Improvement : How to Improve Your Memory in Just 30 Days by Ron White

Persistence & Perseverance: Dance Until It Rains by The Champions Club

The Law of Attraction: How To Get What You Want by Robert Collier

Time Management Tips: 101 Best Ways to Manage Your Time by Lucas McCain

Get Motivated: 101 Best Ways to Get Started, Keep Going and Finish Strong by Lucas McCain

Successful & Healthy Aging: 101 Best Ways to Feel Younger & Live Longer by Lisa J. Johnson

Self Confidence Secrets: How To Be Outgoing and Overcome Shyness by Lucas McCain

Happiness Habits: 21 Secrets to Living a Fun and Outrageously Rewarding Life by Lucas McCain

Self Help Books: The 101 Best Personal Development Classics by Vic Johnson

Overcoming Fear: 101 Best Ways to Overcome Fear and Anxiety and Take Control of Your Life Today! by Lucas McCain

Public Speaking Fear? 21 Secrets To Succeed In Front of Any Crowd by Lucas McCain

Going Green : 101 Ways To Save A Buck While You Save The Earth by Lucas McCain

Stress Management : 101 Best Ways to Relieve Stress and Really Live Life by Lucas McCain

Should I Divorce? 11 Questions To Answer Before You Decide to Stay or Go by Jennifer Jessica

Divorce Recovery: 101 Best Ways To Cope, Heal And Create A Fabulous Life After a Divorce by Lisa J. Johnson

Should I Have a Baby? 10 Questions to Answer BEFORE You Get Pregnant by Jennifer Jessica

Stop Procrastinating: 101 Best Ways to Overcome Procrastination NOW! by Lucas McCain

Think and Grow Rich : The Lost Secret by Vic Johnson

Should I Get Married ? 10 Questions to Answer Before You Say I Do by Jennifer Jessica

How To Attract a Woman: The Secret Handbook of What Women Want in a Man by Jennifer Jessica

Why We Fail: The 101 Best Ways to Overcome Failure and Achieve Success by M. William Hall

Cure Anxiety Now! 21 Ways To Instantly Relieve Anxiety & Stop Panic Attacks by Lucas McCain

Cut Your Debts Now: How To Get Out of Debt Quicker Than You Think by Lucas McCain and Tommi Pryor

Fast NLP Training: Persuasion Techniques To Easily Get What You Want by Lucas McCain

How To Argue: 21 Ways to Win An Argument Without Losing a Friend by Lucas McCain

Meditation Techniques: How To Meditate For Beginners And Beyond by Lucas McCain

How To Become Smarter: 21 Ways to Increase Your Brain Power in the Next 30 Days by M. William Hall

How To Make Extra Money: 100 Perfect Businesses for Part-Time and Retirement Income by Vic Johnson and Tommi Pryor

Should I Do What I Love Or What Makes Money? Why Not Do Both! by Lucas McCain